ORCA
FOOTPRINTS

Take Shelter
AT HOME AROUND THE WORLD

NIKKI TATE & DANI TATE-STRATTON

ORCA BOOK PUBLISHERS

Library and Archives Canada Cataloguing in Publication

Tate, Nikki, 1962-, author
Take shelter : at home around the world / Nikki Tate and
Dani Tate-Stratton.
(Orca footprints)

Includes bibliographical references and index.
Issued in print and electronic formats.
ISBN 978-1-4598-0742-6 (bound).—ISBN 978-1-4598-0743-3 (pdf).—
ISBN 978-1-4598-0744-0 (epub)

1. Dwellings—Juvenile literature. 2. Architecture, Domestic—
Juvenile literature. I. Tate-Stratton, Danielle, 1987-, author
II. Title. III. Series: Orca footprints

GT172.T38 2014   j392.3'6   c2014-901580-1
                      c2014-901581-X

First published in the United States, 2014
Library of Congress Control Number: 2014935384

Summary: Homes around the world reflect the diversity and ingenuity of their residents.

Orca Book Publishers is dedicated to preserving the environment and has printed this book on Forest Stewardship Council® certified paper.

Orca Book Publishers gratefully acknowledges the support for its publishing programs provided by the following agencies: the Government of Canada through the Canada Book Fund and the Canada Council for the Arts, and the Province of British Columbia through the BC Arts Council and the Book Publishing Tax Credit.

Cover images by Getty Images and Shutterstock
Back cover images (top left to right): Getty Images, Getty Images,
Vetsch Architektur (bottom left to right): Corbis Images,
Getty Images, Getty Images

Design and production by Teresa Bubela and Jenn Playford

ORCA BOOK PUBLISHERS
www.orcabook.com

Printed and bound in Canada.

18 17 16 15 • 5 4 3 2

Two young boys from Rajasthan, India, sit in front of their house. Note the thatch roof and mud or cob walls. These thick walls help insulate against temperature fluctuations. BARTOSZ HADYNIAK/GETTY.COM

For T—may our personalities always be at peace. And for Brandy—for as long as our paths may cross, know the effect ripples much longer. All my love and many thanks. —DTS

For Luke—with many thanks for fueling the creative fires! —NT

Contents

CHAPTER ONE:
IN THE GROUND

CHAPTER TWO:
ON THE MOVE

CHAPTER THREE:
HOUSES THAT LIVE AND BREATHE

CHAPTER FOUR:
INNOVATION

Introduction

The phrase Home, Sweet Home *reminds us that a house is more than just a place to fall asleep each night.* PIXELROBOT/
DREAMSTIME.COM

Unpacking familiar books always makes somewhere new feel like home.
DANI TATE-STRATTON

Walls. A door. Windows. A roof. All houses have these basic components and provide shelter from the elements and a place for people to eat, sleep and socialize. From sprawling mansions to precarious cliff dwellings, the variation in what we humans call home is staggering. When I was growing up, my family moved a lot, so by the time I was in high school I had lived in more than fifty places, from a high-rise apartment in a big city to a tiny cabin in the mountains.

With all that packing and unpacking, settling in and moving on, I've had lots of time to think about all the different kinds of places people set up, organize, and move into when they are making a home for themselves and their families. I love seeing how people all over the world build houses that are energy efficient, use local materials and are both beautiful to look at and comfortable to live in.

Humans have always experimented with different building materials like straw, reeds, clay, concrete, brick, glass and modern composite materials like carbon fiber. Some houses today are built with innovative new materials while others ingeniously repurpose used material and use smart design to create efficient and environmentally sensitive spaces.

In *Take Shelter* we'll visit homes all over the world to see how people create that special place where they hang their hats, whether underground or in outer space. So open the door, come on in and make yourself at home!

Extravagant castles like Neuschwanstein in Germany are often tourist attractions today but were once family homes. Imagine how hard it would be to find a toy if you weren't sure which of the 200 rooms you had left it in! EG004713/DREAMSTIME.COM

My Place

When I moved back to Vancouver Island after studying and working in Japan, I wanted to have my own space while still living on the family farm. I set my sights on the pigeon coop 50 meters from the house. The homeowners before us used to keep racing pigeons and had built them a lovely 2 meter by 8 meter shed in which to live. My grampa and I spent several months cleaning, insulating, putting in real walls and making sure it was nice and snug for people, not pigeons. Now it's the perfect bedroom and hangout space away from the house, and I always get a giggle out of telling people that I live in an abandoned pigeon coop. (DTS)

Renovating the pigeon coop was my first introduction to power tools, but I sure learned a lot! Years later, every time I go inside I still feel proud that I helped build my home with my own hands.
E. COLIN WILLIAMS

7

CHAPTER ONE

In the Ground

SNUG AS A BUG IN A...CAVE

A pre-existing hollow in the ground or cliff must have seemed a welcome place to stay for early peoples in need of shelter during the Stone Age (Paleolithic Era). Though this period is long gone (estimates vary from about 40,000 to 2 million years ago), even today many people live in caves or underground dwellings, using the Earth as their main protection from the elements.

According to archaeologists, there are two types of cave dwelling: the *cliff house*, which is built onto platforms on a cliff, and the *cavete*, which makes use of existing recesses or openings.

Families have lived in these cave houses for hundreds of years. MATHES/DREAMSTIME.COM

WAY BACK WHEN...IN IRAN

Many cave homes have long been abandoned, but not all cave dwellings are architectural relics. In Iran, at the foot of Mount Sahand, people have been living in a village named Kandovan for centuries. One of just a handful of cave villages continuously inhabited to this day, Kandovan is built into deposits made by a now-dormant volcano. Cone-shaped pillars of rock were left in

These rocks in Turkey were hollowed out to create cave cities. ELENA YAKUSHEVA/DREAMSTIME.COM

the wake of its previous explosions and have become home to many generations of family members.

A typical home in this region has four stories. Animals are kept on the ground level, while people sleep and live on the second and third stories. The fourth level is used for storage. The buildings have been modernized over the years and now include amenities like electricity.

KEKULI HOUSES

The Interior Salish people of British Columbia traditionally built a winter house called a *kekuli*. These homes are partially underground, which helps keep them warm during cold weather. Logs span an excavated area and provide support for the roof covering of strips of cedar bark, grass or pine needles, and earth.

HOME FACT: Though it sounds a bit like a type of dinosaur, the word *troglodyte* actually refers to a person who lives in a cave or belongs to a cave-dwelling community. The residents of Kandovan are modern-day troglodytes.

Kekuli houses like this one provide low-profile protection from the elements.
THE KINGFISHER INTERPRETIVE CENTRE

HOME FACT: Over 40 million people live in underground houses in the neighboring northern provinces of Shaanxi and Shanxi in China. That's more than the entire population of Canada!

Houses like these (known as *pit houses*) can be found all over the world. The oldest pit house is believed to be in the Central Ukraine. The wall and roof supports are made of mammoth bones!

LUXURY LIVING UNDERGROUND

During the Cold War that started after World War II and lasted through the 1980s, many people in North America and Russia (then known as the USSR) were convinced that a nuclear war was going to happen and the world would become uninhabitable because of radiation poisoning. Some people believed that by building homes underground they could survive the initial nuclear attack and wait until the worst of the radiation had dissipated before emerging from their safe havens to rebuild society.

In Las Vegas, a two-bedroom home is hidden eight meters (twenty-six feet) below ground, underneath a normal-looking

My Place

When I visited my father's family home in England, I was surprised to see a small, curved building made of corrugated iron in a neighbor's backyard. The hut was being used to store garden tools, but when my father was a child, many families in England had little huts called Anderson Shelters in their gardens. Bomb shelters like these protected people during air raids and were equipped with blankets, tinned food and water. Families also stored games in the shelters so there was something to keep children entertained. Small stoves were used to heat food and keep everyone warm. Oil lamps and candles were the most common sources of light. (NT)

The sturdy huts were erected and then buried under a thick layer of dirt so they could be used as bomb shelters during World War II. MARTIN STANLEY

house in the suburbs. The underground house has a false sky, a swimming pool, a putting green and a barbecue disguised as a massive boulder. A sophisticated ventilation and air purification system is meant to keep the atmosphere breathable, even after a disastrous attack, and of course there is lots of room to store canned goods, water and other food and supplies in case it isn't safe to venture above ground.

Even if a global disaster is not on the horizon, there are many advantages to building a home partially or completely underground. Temperature control is easy with an underground home. In the summer, things tend to stay cool, and in the winter, the warmth stored in the ground during the hot months gently warms the interior. Some homes that are built completely underground become almost invisible, and it's possible to use the roof (which is actually at ground level) to increase the space available for growing food crops. Light floods into a well-designed buried home through light tunnels and by taking advantage of a slope to build many windows into downhill-facing walls.

Stone mason Joe Thompson used 120 tonnes of stone, most of it from local sources, to build a Hobbit-inspired house on Vancouver Island.
BRUCE STOTESBURY, TIMES COLONIST

This group of nine houses is built around an artificial pond in Dietikon, Switzerland, and includes indoor and outdoor living space as well as shared underground parking. VETSCH ARCHITEKTUR AG

LIVING (WAY) DOWN UNDER

One of the settlements taking advantage of earth as a natural insulator can be found in Coober Pedy, Australia, an opal-mining town with 1,700 residents. Since extensive underground networks were already in place from the old opal mines, it was a logical step for locals to move underground to escape the intense summer heat of the Australian Outback. Temperatures in the area regularly climb over 40 degrees Celsius (about 100 degrees Fahrenheit). While not all residents live underground, the network of "dugouts" is extensive and also features several underground churches, a jewelry store, a bar and—in one house—an underground swimming pool. These homes are also good for the environment, as they have a much smaller *carbon footprint* (the amount of carbon your actions release into the atmosphere) than that of a traditional home.

The Catholic Church of Saint Peter and Saint Paul is completely underground, giving the residents of Coober Pedy a unique—and temperate—place to worship. YAROSLAV SOROKOTYAGA/DREAMSTIME.COM

NESTLED UNDER A GREEN ROOF

Houses dug into the ground can be easily covered by a "green" or "living" roof, which uses plant material and requires several layers, each with a particular function. To stop water from dripping through after a heavy rain (or after the roof gets watered), a waterproof membrane protects the inside of the building. Plants need soil to grow, but soil can be heavy, particularly when it gets waterlogged. Special lightweight planting mixes provide plants with nutrition and support for their roots, and strike a balance between holding enough water so plants don't dry out and draining well enough that the plants don't drown.

Vegetables, herbs, grasses, moss and decorative plants can all be grown on correctly prepared rooftops. A green roof provides excellent insulation and helps modulate the temperature inside the building. TONYTHETIGER/WIKIPEDIA.ORG

LIVING ROUGH IN LAS VEGAS

People who are desperate for housing sometimes have to look beyond the traditional four walls and a roof for ideas.

A family sits down to eat in their fairy chimney (a type of rock formation) in Cappadocia, Turkey.
BOISVIEUX CHRISTOPHE/HEMIS.FR/GETTY.COM

Residents of the underground tunnels go to great lengths to make their living areas as homey as possible. AUSTIN HARGRAVE

For as many as 1,000 homeless people in Las Vegas, the extensive network of storm drain tunnels has become their home. Tunnel residents, including couples, children and their pets, create living spaces of up to 37 square meters (400 square feet) with furniture and household supplies gathered from the streets of the city. While the tunnel dwellers are able to take advantage of pre-existing structures that include floors, a roof and walls, as well as electrical outlets for small appliances, there are obvious drawbacks to such a living situation.

Given that the purpose of these underground tunnels, which are hundreds of kilometers in length, is to drain water away from the city and prevent flooding, underground residents are in constant danger of flash floods. Water levels can rise up to thirty centimeters (twelve inches) per minute, and personal belongings are often kept in crates for easy transfer to high shelves.

My Place

Our house, built in the 1950s, has a mysterious little room we've always jokingly called "the bomb shelter." Given its location in the basement, it was probably built as a root cellar. When I started learning how to make cheese, I read about how the best cheese makers use caves for aging wheels of cheese before they are ready to eat. Perfect! I thought, and moved my cheddar right in, where it aged with great success. It was great to finally find the perfect job for that funny little room. (DTS)

The mysterious room under the front steps has some cavelike properties—always cool with a consistently higher humidity than the rest of the house.
NIKKI TATE

It's far from ideal to live in a place where water streams along the floor, it's nearly always dark, and creatures like crayfish and rats share your home. However, directly beneath the glittering lights of Las Vegas's famous Strip, this parallel world in the storm tunnels provides relative safety and stability for residents.

344 DAYS UNDERGROUND

The record for the longest time spent continuously dwelling in a cave without emerging at all is 344 days. In World War II, Jewish people across Europe were being persecuted, and several Ukrainian families took refuge in an extremely long cave known as Priest's Grotto.

Of course, if you are hiding in a large cave, too scared to emerge for fear of capture, it would be difficult to know when to come out. Eventually, a kind farmer left a note in a glass bottle that he tossed near the mouth of the cave. On the note he wrote, *The Germans have already gone.* Some of these same friendly farmers helped sustain the families by selling food to them, but other neighbors launched attacks on those hiding in the caves, making their eventual survival even more miraculous. In fact, only 1 percent of Jewish families survived World War II in Ukraine, and the cave is credited with being critical to saving many of those lives.

It must have been quite a shock for those who re-emerged into the light after so long. It's unpleasant enough for your eyes when someone turns on the light and interrupts your sleep. Now imagine your eyes haven't seen natural light—and in fact have rarely seen the light of candles—for nearly a year. For one young girl, it was also very confusing. Four-year-old Pepkala Blitzer later recalled asking her parents to turn off the bright candle—she had forgotten what the sun was like and couldn't remember ever having seen it.

HOME FACT: In a cave, you can make water from air! Caves can be damp, which isn't ideal for human habitation. To get around this problem, one family in Festus, Missouri, uses dehumidifiers to pull up to 380 liters (about 100 gallons) of water per day from the air in their cave home, which they then recycle for their plants, animals and garden.

Thirty-eight people evaded the Nazis by hiding in this cave for 344 days during World War II. PETER LANE TAYLOR

CHAPTER TWO

On the Move

Nomads like these women from Morocco still live much as they would have a hundred years ago. DEVY/DREAMSTIME.COM

EARLY SHELTERS

Until about 8,000 years ago, many cultures around the world were nomadic, with families roaming across the land in search of food. Because they were often on the move, they had to find places to shelter at night and in bad weather. Sometimes these early people slept in caves, and sometimes they erected simple shelters that could be moved from place to place. In the far north, shelters were built using the only material on hand—snow! Elsewhere, reeds, sticks and animal hides were used to keep the rain out and to protect those inside from hungry predators.

For some of today's families, living on a sailboat or in a camperized van is something to be done for a few months or years while exploring the world. For many nomadic children, though, it's a way of life. They move from place to place with their families—and with their homes.

FOLLOWING THE HERDS

A community's lifestyle dictates the kind of housing it uses. For herders who must move grazing livestock to good pasture according to the season, portable housing is essential.

A *ger* is a small house with curved walls used by the Mongols of Central Asia. These nomadic herders have lived in similar houses for at least three thousand years. Ger walls are made of a latticework of sticks on top of which sits a roof designed a bit like the spokes of a wheel. The walls are prevented from springing outward by strong, tight bands wrapped around the exterior.

Traditionally, families who live in houses like these keep flocks of sheep, goats and horses, so it makes sense that the walls are insulated with felt and wool made from these animals. When it's time to relocate, the whole house is taken apart and loaded onto yaks or camels to be moved to the next location.

Tipis are portable homes traditionally used by Native North Americans from the Great Plains. Covering these cone-shaped structures with animal hides keep tipis warm in winter,

HOME FACT:
In Mongolia, a yurt is called a ger. The English translation means "home." Many people in Mongolia still live in gers.

A ger in Dadal, Mongolia, the birthplace of Genghis Khan, who united the nomadic tribes of northeast Asia. DIETER MEYRL/ISTOCK.COM

17

In the late 1800s, these Piegan children lived in what is now Montana. They would have helped to move their tipi home from place to place.

cool in the summer and nice and dry in times of rain. Like
gers, tipis can be dismantled, moved to a new location and
constructed quickly. The poles, 3.5 to 4.5 meters (12 to 15 feet)
long, used to make the frame of a tipi are called *lodge poles*.

ROLLING DOWN THE ROAD

The Romany (Romani) people of Europe love their sturdy,
strong horses. Quiet and reliable, these horses pull wooden
caravans that are sometimes called *vardos* or wagons. The
designs vary, but the fanciest are like works of art with elabo-
rate wooden carvings and intricate paintwork or gold leaf deco-
ration. Inside, each caravan contains sleeping bunks, a kitchen
area with a cast-iron stove, and storage in shelves and drawers.

What you won't find in a traditional vardo is a toilet, consid-
ered too unclean to have inside. Instead, Romany families stay
in regular stopping places where they share permanent bathroom facilities.

ALL ABOARD!

Imagine living in a house just 12 meters long, 4 meters wide
and 2 meters tall (40 feet long, 13 feet wide and 6.5 feet tall),
where every step you take is a wobbly one, and you never know
just what will turn up outside your window. That's what life
is like if you live on a sailboat. Some liveaboards stay moored
at marinas, but others travel from city to city and country to
country on journeys that can last months, years or decades.

People who are about to do a long offshore cruise provision
(stock up) before setting sail. Since boats move up and down,
to even in calm water, sailors try to make sure everything that
could break, or is heavy enough to hurt someone if it came
flying out of a cupboard, is tied in or tied down.

*A travois is a simple sledlike frame in the shape
of a triangle used for moving loads over the
ground. Native Americans used a couple of tipi
lodge poles to make a travois pulled by a horse
or a dog.* GLENBOW ARCHIVES NA-395-8

*Vardos are both portable and beautiful—imagine
living right inside a work of art!*
CLEARVISTA/DREAMSTIME.COM

Many sailing families with children take schoolwork along, and often the places they visit become their classrooms.
SARA DAWN JOHNSON

HOME FACT: The little chimney that vents smoke from the woodstove inside a Romany wagon is always on the right side of the roof. That way, the chimney is less likely to be damaged by a low branch when the wagon is driven along the left side of the road, as is usual in Great Britain.

Living on a ship like The World *lets you travel without leaving your home.*
STUART PEARCEY/DREAMSTIME.COM

GONE CRUISING!

Have you ever been on a cruise ship? For lots of families, a week on the high seas is an amazing way to vacation. Restaurants, shops, movie theaters and even ice rinks and bowling alleys are built aboard fancy modern cruise ships. "Wouldn't it be nice to live here all the time?" is a question many people ask as they get off the ship on the final day. For some lucky people, a luxury cruise ship named *The World* is their home. With only 165 staterooms, it's a bit like a floating apartment building that comes complete with coffee shops and restaurants, pools, a gym and even a grocery store! Of course, the backyard changes all the time. One day you might wake up in Istanbul, Turkey, and another you could be in Tokyo, Japan. All of that pampered traveling comes with a cost though—it's rumored that the monthly fees are about the same as what it costs to buy a small car!

AT HOME ON THE ROAD

Romany vardos need a horse or two to move them from place to place, and Mongolian families rely on their camels and yaks to transport their gers, but it's common to find homes that are also forms of transportation themselves. Some motorhomes and camperized vans are designed and built to move themselves from place to place, while travel trailers are towed behind another vehicle. Inside, these homes on wheels make excellent use of space. Sleeping bunks are often converted to dining or sitting areas during the day. Stoves and sinks can be covered to make the most of the limited counter space in tiny kitchens.

Some mobile homes begin their lives as other kinds of vehicles. School buses can be bought for a relatively low price and then fitted out with all the luxuries of home. If you have a portable profession—like being a writer or graphic designer—converting a school bus or other vehicle allows you to add features that best suit your lifestyle.

People have built amazing portable homes in unusual vehicles, some much smaller than a bus. Enterprising people have built tiny homes inside ambulances and fire trucks and even on the back of a bicycle.

FLY AWAY HOME

For travelers, airplanes can be cramped and uncomfortable. Living on a plane seems like the *last* thing anyone would want to do! But take out all the seats and overhead compartments, put in some walls and a bed, and a retired plane can make a perfectly respectable home. Plane homes are often suspended in the air or rest on a pedestal system, giving them the impression of still being in flight. Keeping the aircraft on the ground on its original landing gear means the huge shock absorbers act as an earthquake safety system,

Known as "skoolies," converted school buses have a surprising amount of room, especially when the roof is used for storage.
JOHN SFONDILIAS/DREAMSTIME.COM

Thanks to folding furniture and very careful use of space, this tiny home includes a sink, stove and bathtub, all of which collapse into the front wall for storage.
PEOPLE'S INDUSTRIAL DESIGN OFFICE, PEOPLE'S ARCHITECTURE OFFICE

HOME FACT: Not all homes on water move. A float home is built on a stable platform and is not meant to travel. A houseboat has a hull and some sort of engine and steering but is designed for comfort and space rather than speed and maneuverability. Canal boats and barges may have an engine, but they don't generally leave the protected watery pathways of canals and slow-moving rivers.

This suspended plane has been converted into a hotel, giving visitors the illusion of flying through the Costa Rican jungle as they sleep.
VINCENT CASTELLO/WWW.COSTAVERDE.COM

helping to absorb the rattle and roll of an earthquake. Airplane fuselages can also handle winds up to 925 kilometers per hour (575 miles per hour), making them great refuges in hurricane-prone areas.

At about 93 square meters (1,000 square feet), a Boeing 727 (one of the popular sizes for refurbishment) doesn't give you a huge amount of living space by North American standards, but because of the cargo deck there is loads of room for your belongings underneath your living area! With some good fencing, you could even turn the wings into a wing-top garden accessed through emergency exit doors.

There are some unique design challenges though—ceilings aren't very high and walls are curved, so most of the furniture needs to be custom made.

My Place

When I was a kid, my family bought a camper that fit on the back of our car. Two people could sleep in a bunk in the part of the camper that stretched over the roof of the car. Everywhere we went, curious people asked us questions about our unusual accommodations. Many wanted to know if we were traveling with an outhouse stuck on the back of our car, and one man thought the odd addition was for a horse! (NT)

Unfortunately, I don't have any photos of our funny car camper, but this newer model is similar in design. LIFTARN/WIKIMEDIA.ORG

HOUSES THAT YOU MOVE TO: HOTELS

Though some people do live in hotels all the time, hotel rooms are designed to be temporary homes for travelers on the go. Many hotels are a bit beige and boring, but some are doing everything they can to make their guests feel special or offer a unique experience.

Chill out

In Sweden, the world's first ice hotel, in Jukkasjärvi, opened in 1990 and has been rebuilt each year ever since. Only open from mid-December to mid-April, the hotel literally disappears each spring when the walls melt away! Visitors tucked into warm sleeping bags sleep on beds made with blocks of ice and covered with reindeer hides.

Capsule hotels

In Japan, small and efficient hotels are quite common around major business centers where workers might not finish work before the last train. Rooms measure just 2 meters (6 feet, 7 inches) long, 1 meter (3 feet, 3 inches) wide and 1.2 meters (4 feet, 1 inch) high and barely let you sit up. To make the most of the available space, these capsules are stacked two high and several wide. If you are on the upper level, you climb a ladder to get into bed just inches from your neighbors. Each capsule features a bed, TV and wireless Internet connection, and shared bathrooms aren't too far away. The small size also means a small bill. Rooms like these can cost less than a tenth the price of a regular hotel room.

Prison hotels

For a creepy stay, what about a prison hotel? The Karosta Prison Hotel in Liepaja, Latvia, promises to be "unfriendly, unheated and uncomfortable." It's a good thing the cost of the room includes a promise to let you out the next day!

There are several ice hotels to chill out in around the world, including the Hotel de Glace in Quebec City, Canada. MARIE HAVENS/ SHUTTERSTOCK.COM

In Japanese capsule hotels, miniature rooms are just big enough to slide yourself in to sleep. WETBACK/ISTOCKPHOTO.COM

Malmaison Oxford, a fancy hotel in England, lets visitors stay in what were once prison cells, with none of the discomfort of a night in jail. M L LEA BELLAS

BUILDING WITH SUPERSIZED BLOCKS

Shipping containers spend their working lives on the move. After retirement, some find new jobs as housing. Many shipping container homes are simple. Holes for doors and windows are cut in the steel walls of the container. Inside, walls are framed in to divide up the living space. With basic carpentry skills, it's not difficult to build a home like this for a relatively small amount of money, particularly if you are good at recycling building materials.

Architects have also recognized the potential for using these sturdy building blocks. Shipping container homes don't have to be small or plain. Modern, spacious homes can be made by stacking or joining together several shipping containers. By cutting holes in floors, ceilings and walls, it's possible to move

Shipping containers can be used to make modern homes like this one. GUBGIB/SHUTTERSTOCK.COM

between levels and create spaces much larger than you'd expect when starting with boxes only 2.4 to 3 meters (8 to 10 feet) wide.

Reusing a sturdy, weatherproof structure like a shipping container is also an economical way to provide housing for the homeless. In Campbell River on Vancouver Island in British Columbia, a shipping container was converted into a movable shelter with eight rooms. Each room has two beds, a smoke detector, light and heat. Powered by a diesel generator, the shelter can be towed and parked in a convenient location. In Campbell River, a local church provides supervision during the hours the shelter is open. A storage shed is available so those who use the shelter can safely store their belongings.

This Campbell River homeless shelter is open from 7 PM to 7 AM and provides a safe place to sleep. RON KERR, CAMPBELL RIVER, BC

My Place

I've always dreamed of living in a castle. When I was nineteen, I set off on a backpacking trip to Europe. I camped or stayed in youth hostels, which provide inexpensive accommodations all over the world. When I hiked up a steep hill from the train station to the youth hostel in Culrain, Scotland, I was astonished to see that the hostel was located in a lovely old castle. Carbisdale Castle had statues and art on display in the grand entry hall, a shared kitchen for visitors to use and bicycles to rent. Even though it was said to be haunted, the only others I saw during my stay were backpackers! (NT)

The grand entry hall was a welcome surprise when I arrived in Culrain!
RICARDO FRANTZ/WIKIPEDIA.ORG

CHAPTER THREE

Houses that Live and Breathe

MESSY, MARVELOUS MUD!

Imagine turning some of the mud pies you made on the playground into full-sized homes! That's sort of what natural builders do when they use straw, clay, mud and other natural materials to build houses. Instead of being square and precise like most houses in North America, natural buildings are often round and curvy. Natural builders sometimes joke that they measure in "round feet" and not square feet or meters.

Unlike regular buildings, which have walls about 15 centimeters (6 inches) thick, natural buildings are often 46 centimeters (18 inches) or more from outside to inside! Thicker walls mean straw bales don't have to be cut into smaller sizes and the buildings are naturally insulated. They are also usually very quiet inside.

Many natural builders are also artists—stained and colored glass, sculpted walls and colorful lime plasters (used in place of paint) are common. Each house is unique to the builder. One natural builder can often recognize the style of another in the same way it's possible to recognize a particular painter by their brushstrokes and the colors they use.

Everyone can build a house when it comes to using cob. Getting your hands into the mix is lots of fun! O.U.R. ECOVILLAGE

Young children in India sit in front of a hut made with a thick thatch roof. IMAGES BAZAAR/GETTY.COM

WHAT'S UP TOP?

A roof keeps residents dry and warm or cool and shaded. Roofs can be made from a wide range of materials. In the past, the choice of building material was often determined by what could be found close by.

Thatched roofs are made with dried vegetation. Depending on where the house is built, the roof might be made with layers of straw, reeds or heather (in Great Britain and several European countries), ti leaves (Hawaii), or fan palms (Fiji). Thatched roofs are layered so that water sheds away from the building underneath.

HOME FACT: It takes approximately 11,800 kilograms (13 US tons) of straw to build a 93-square-meter (1,000-square-foot) straw bale house. That's about 575 bales of straw grown on approximately 2 hectares (5 acres) of land.

This house on Mayne Island in British Columbia features a mural done by friends and in-wall storage for jars right beside the stove. Using the deep walls for storage is a great strategy. DANI TATE-STRATTON

HOME FACT: Although natural home builders like to use cob to build whole houses, many people start with smaller projects like benches and outdoor ovens.

This hut in Tiébélé, Burkina Faso, is made from adobe (mud brick) and decorated with traditional tribal paintings. BERNARDO ERTL/ DREAMSTIME.COM

NATURAL BUILDING

For many people around the world, natural building simply means traditional building. While still a novelty in North America, rammed earth buildings are the traditional homes of the Hmong in Vietnam. The first rammed earth buildings were found in China and date back to 5000 BCE.

Cob houses

Cob buildings (made of a mix of sand, clay, water, straw and dirt) have been around for a very long time. Cob, or *tabya*, has been used in northern Africa and Spain since the eleventh century. Even today, fans of cob like to mix the basic ingredients with their bare feet, a technique that natural builders swear works better than any other!

Keeping the mud away

If natural building walls are made from a mix of materials like dirt and animal dung, how do people do things like shower without turning their houses to mud? *Tadelakt* (pronounced *tat-eh-lak)* is used where the walls need to be waterproof. The technique originated in Morocco where, in the local Berber language, the word *tadelakt* means "to rub." That's probably because a lot of rubbing is required to make good tadelakt! Once it is mixed and on the wall, the lime plaster is smoothed and compressed, first with a hard, flat stone, and then with a trowel. Finally, a mixture of olive oil and soap is rubbed into the walls, helping to waterproof them and adding a beautiful shine.

A dirt floor is not dirty

One of the common types of flooring in natural buildings or simple dwellings is dirt. This doesn't mean you are living on bare ground. Earthen floors are just as carefully prepared as the rest of the house and are made from soil, straw and clay. Once installed, they are sealed with plant-based oils like hemp or linseed oil, or with beeswax, and are then waterproof enough to be mopped.

Rammed earth walls

Have you ever played with the sand art toy where you pour colored sand into empty plastic frames or bottles one layer at a time to make pretty designs and patterns? Natural builders use a similar technique, but on a much larger scale, when they build rammed earth walls. A single wall of this type is often used as an accent piece in a naturally built house. Rammed earth walls are often made of layers of red, orange, yellow, brown and cream-colored earth. To make a wall like this, first a frame, or formwork, is built. Next, a damp mixture of sand, gravel and clay is poured into the form. To make it more attractive, the different layers might be colored with natural pigments. Once the earth is in the form, it is tamped down to compress it and make it stick together as a solid wall.

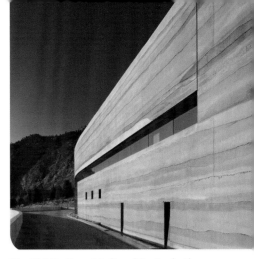

The Nk'Mip Desert Cultural Centre in the Okanagan region of British Columbia welcomes visitors with a rammed earth wall that incorporates local soils into its design.
COURTESY OF THE NDCC

THE THREE Rs: REDUCE, REUSE, RECYCLE

Most natural builders try their best to reuse as many materials as possible. Some houses are made almost entirely of recycled materials. Used car tires, for example, can be used to build foundations and walls. This type of building is known as an Earthship building.

Dressing your naturally built house in recycled clothes

It's said that a naturally built house needs good boots and a good hat to survive. In building terms, the hat is the roof, which needs to overhang the walls of the house by 0.6 meters (2 feet) to keep everything nice and dry. Its boots are the foundation, which comes up at least 0.6 meters (2 feet) above ground level. Urbanite, which is made of old sidewalks and other concrete things that have been demolished, is commonly used for foundations. Stacking the chunks of urbanite and gluing the rubble in place with cement, cob or plaster, ensures the foundation walls are solid and strong without the need to make new concrete.

Children in Iqaluit, NWT, take part in an igloo-building contest for children. How would you do? WOLFGANG KAEHLER/CORBIS.COM

WHAT'S ON HAND?

Using building materials found locally makes a lot of sense. There's no need to ship logs from a thousand miles away when you live right beside a quarry and could use stone to build a lovely house. Even in places where there might not seem to be a lot of building resources, houses can be built using materials like reeds, straw or even snow!

Igluit

Traditionally built by Canada's northern Inuit and Greenland's Thule people, an igloo (plural: igluit) is a domed dwelling constructed with ice and snow. Air pockets trapped in snow mean igluit are surprisingly warm and efficient. Some builders add animal hides to the inside of the igloo, making them even warmer. An igloo can be built in just a few hours out of free and readily available materials, which makes it perfectly suited to the harsh environment of the Far North.

My Place

When I was a kid my brother and I spent a lot of time building houses out of whatever we had handy. In Australia we made a playhouse out of cardboard boxes under a lemon tree. In Fort McMurray we built several pretty cool tree houses. In Banff we tried many times to build a real igloo but never quite figured out how to stop the roof from caving in! (NT)

Many of our games as children revolved around building houses and forts.
HELGA WILLIAMS

Longhouses

Iroquois longhouses start with a framework of young, thin trees pushed into the ground in parallel rows. The tops of these trees are then bent toward each other to make a long, gently arched structure. Covered with strips of bark peeled from elm trees, the houses can be added to at the ends each time a newly married couple joins the clan. Platforms and shelves along the long walls provide storage space for food, clothing and bedding.

A longhouse might be more than 90 meters (300 feet) long and could shelter several families. PHOTOGRAPH COURTESY OF SAINTE-MARIE AMONG THE HURONS, MIDLAND, ONTARIO

Tree houses

Lots of kids like climbing trees, but sitting up in a tree can be a bit uncomfortable. Adding a platform and maybe a ladder of some kind to make it easier to get in and out of the tree creates the most basic kind of tree house. Why stop there?

Kids are not the only ones who enjoy looking at the world from up in a tree. Some tree houses are very fancy with many rooms and all the features of homes built closer to the ground.

Several hotels around the world are built high up in the trees. One of the most famous is the Treetops Hotel in Kenya. Originally, there were only two guest rooms built overlooking a watering hole so visitors had an excellent view of African animals coming to drink. As interest and demand grew, more rooms were added, but the hotel was still small when it burned down in 1954. It was rebuilt in 1957 in a chestnut tree, and today there are about fifty rooms.

Houses on stilts

What if you lived in a place where the river flooded every year, or near an ocean that created huge waves in your town during hurricane season? Stilt houses, also called *palafitte* or pile dwellings, are found in Europe, Asia and the Americas. Commonly used building materials include bamboo, rope, straw and wood, sometimes reinforced with concrete. They are usually about three meters (ten feet) off the ground to allow for flooding, and may be connected by bridges.

The Alnwick Garden Treehouse in Northumberland, England, is made from four types of wood and features an educational room and restaurant. GAIL JOHNSON/DREAMSTIME.COM

When the risk of flooding is lower, the space underneath the house can be used for working, socializing or storage. Raising the living space off the ground also provides some protection from animals and vermin.

Reed houses

Reed houses in southern Iraq are built completely with tall reeds that grow in the marshes fed by water from the lower Euphrates River. The tallest, thickest bundles of reeds form support pillars and columns, and reed mats fill in the walls. This type of building is now rare, as the marshlands have mostly been destroyed by draining water from the Euphrates.

These reed houses float on the surface of Lake Titicaca in Peru and are inhabited by the Uros people.
CMUNOZJUGO-EMRE SAFAK/WIKIPEDIA.ORG

MOUNTAINTOP LIVING

Other cultures have built up and up—way up into the Himalayan Mountains of Nepal, Tibet, Bhutan and India. At the Phuktal Monastery in India, about seventy monks live high in the mountains in a dwelling built in the form of a honeycomb. Established in the twelfth century, the small, connected rooms of the monastery appear to be carved out of the side of the mountain and are built in what seems to be a random pattern. In fact, the layout makes the best use of the available space.

In areas like this, where the altitude is higher, building materials change because of the environment around the house. At a certain altitude or temperature, trees can no longer grow, so far less timber is likely to be used than in the buildings of jungle or forest communities. This is why it's more common to use rock and clay to build homes high in the mountains.

WHAT'S KEEPING YOU WARM?

In most climates, insulation is important to keep the house warm in the winter or cool in the summer. Most commercial insulation is made of fiberglass or Styrofoam, but there are some other interesting materials with great insulating properties. Whole sheep fleeces, recycled blue jeans, seedling containers, corn cobs and recycled paper are all examples of recycled insulation.

Ecovative Design is a company that has created a natural alternative to polystyrene insulation. By combining agricultural waste like corn stalks with fast-growing fungal tissue (*mycelium*, the non-fruiting, rootlike part of mushrooms), insulation can literally be grown in place. Sealed inside rigid boards, the mushroom insulation dries in about a month, at which point it is dormant. Non-toxic and fully compostable when no longer needed, this material is also being used as an alternative to plastic packaging.

Children at the Phuktal Monastery in Phuktal/India learn science, math, Hindi, English, written Tibetan, Buddhist philosophy, Sowa-Rigpe (Tibetan medicine) and all aspects of monastic life. EMMY SCHOORL/ WWW.EMMYSCHOORL.COM

The mushroom insulation used in this tiny house was grown right inside its walls! COURTESY OF ECOVATIVEDESIGN.COM

CHAPTER FOUR

Innovation

GET CREATIVE!

Simply finding room for everyone to live comfortably without having to spread out onto farmland or battle difficult climates is a challenge. In some places like Manhattan, New York, the population density is an astonishing 26,717 residents per square kilometer (69,464 residents per square mile). Compare this to an average of 33.82 people in the same area for the United States as a whole. In densely packed cities, one solution is for residents to live up, up in the air, in big, tall apartment buildings.

In Japan, apartment-size furniture takes up only 60 to 70 percent of the space the same piece of furniture would occupy in North America.

In Hong Kong, Gary Chang squeezed twenty-four rooms into his 31-square-meter (336-square-foot) apartment! To get so much space out of such a tiny footprint, he designed an ingenious series of movable walls. Gary Chang isn't the only one with a teeny tiny home. One of the narrowest houses in the world is in Warsaw, Poland. In some places the walls are only 71 centimeters (28 inches) apart! Despite being the width of a hall, the house includes all the basics—a (single) bed, kitchen and bathroom.

Buildings that stretch high into the sky and for as far as the eye can see allow Manhattan to reach its incredibly high population density.
GRIGOR ATANASOV/DREAMSTIME.COM

Another way that people innovate is by finding new ways to push the limits of construction by building the biggest, strongest or longest house. The most expensive house cost more than a billion dollars to build and is in Mumbai, India. It is the size of an apartment building at twenty-seven stories and a staggering 37,161 square meters (400,000 square feet)! It has six levels of underground parking, 600 staff and three helicopter pads! Named Antilia, it was built for Mukesh Ambani, chairman of Reliance Industries, who lives there with his wife, two sons and a daughter.

The walls in Gary Chang's tiny apartment are easily pushed and pulled out of the way to reveal spaces like a linen closet, soaker tub, guest bed and screening room complete with a hammock! EDGE DESIGN INSTITUTE LTD.

AT THE ENDS OF THE EARTH

Challenging environments push designers and engineers to find creative housing solutions. Even though there are no permanent residents on the icy desert that is Antarctica, some 4,000 scientists, photographers and tour guides live on the continent during the summer months. Fewer people stay through the winter, but there are enough families in residence to have a school in one of the settlements.

HOME FACT: The human population density of the entire world is 13.7 per square kilometer (35.62 per square mile). However, if you take out the oceans and Antarctica, that number rises to about 50 people per square kilometer or over 130 people per square mile.

In some ways, the bases in Antarctica are built like large refrigerators, except they work to keep the cold out, not in! JONATHAN LINGEL/DREAMSTIME.COM

How do people live on one of the least forgiving places on Earth, with an average temperature of minus 50 degrees Celsius (minus 58 degrees Fahrenheit)? Facilities at several bases are built partially or completely underground, and during the winter, snow blankets everything, burying buildings and equipment alike.

FLOATING HOME

Polar ice caps, mountaintops, deserts and oceans are all tricky environments in which to live. Nowhere, though, forces residents to be more resourceful than out in space.

The astronauts and cosmonauts living in the International Space Station, or ISS, call a very technologically advanced place their home. But living in an orbiting house means they have some unique problems. All their food (and everything else) floats around! The space is small, and at somewhere between 330 and 435 kilometers (205 and 270 miles) above the Earth, it's not easy to go home when you miss your friends and family. About the same size as one and a half Boeing 747 planes, the ISS is home to six permanent residents and the occasional visitor.

Because water can cause problems if left to float about on its own, even basic chores like showering and tooth brushing can be challenging. Instead of traditional showers, astronauts rely on wipes to get clean and must relearn how to shower so soap and water stay where they belong. Going to the toilet is a similar challenge: a suctioning system keeps everything clean and running smoothly.

To avoid floating around while asleep, astronauts climb into sleeping bags hooked onto the wall, and a shutter system blocks as much light as possible from the sleeping quarters.

Before astronaut Chris Hadfield can slice tomatoes, he first must catch them!
NASA/WIKIMEDIA.ORG

TEMPORARY HOUSING

Back here on Earth, not everyone has a permanent place to call home: good housing can be expensive. For those who are unable to afford a home, small temporary dwellings offer a safe alternative to living on the street.

Design meets housing—in a Dumpster

Recycled materials find new life in small homes built by artist Greg Kloehn. One of his most interesting designs is his teeny-tiny Dumpster house. With a port-a-potty, sun deck, barbecue and outdoor shower, the little house is strong, weatherproof and portable. His other designs make good use of recycled materials, and each is small enough to fit into a parking spot. One of Kloehn's simplest designs uses only five pallets and takes just two or three days to make.

Tiny houses like this could be grouped in small villages on empty lots. By providing communal facilities like showers, toilets and gathering spaces, these villages can offer residents the benefits of community living without having to bear the cost of a full-sized house or apartment.

HOME FACT: Each year, 35 million people are forced to flee their homes because of war, famine, drought or other conflict. Many of these refugees will be forced to seek shelter in a camp or temporary dwelling.

Artist Greg Kloehn gives away these teeny-tiny homes to homeless people in Oakland, California. BRIAN J REYNOLDS

There are many reasons why people might need temporary housing: war, flood, fire, earthquake, famine or other disasters can leave large numbers of people homeless. Often, refugees are housed in tent cities, which do provide basic shelter but are far from ideal when people need to stay put for more than a short time.

IKEA flat pack disaster homes

Working with the United Nations High Commission for Refugees, IKEA has designed small houses that come packed flat in boxes. Each house is 17.5 square meters (188 square feet) and can be put together in about four hours. Solar panels on the roof power built-in lights and provide power for a USB outlet. A special fabric cover stretches over the roof to help reflect the sun's rays during the day and keep heat in overnight. In the past, the tents used in refugee camps lasted an average of six months before starting to disintegrate after exposure to harsh weather conditions. Even though the IKEA shelters are more expensive (the company hopes to be able to build them for about a thousand dollars each), they should last for several years.

Houses like these could provide a more efficient and longer-term form of housing during an emergency. ©IKEA FOUNDATION/ ÅSA SJÖSTRÖM

EFFICIENT HOMES

Emergency shelters are not the only homes that take advantage of new technology to be energy self-sufficient. The IKAROS house was designed and built by the University of Applied Sciences in Rosenheim, Germany. Super-efficient heating and cooling systems, state-of-the-art insulation, solar panels and natural ventilation all contribute to the home being so energy efficient. The design of the exterior walls helps to shade the building during the hot months and passively collects sunlight during cooler weather.

Solar power is one way to make a home more energy efficient, but energy for heat, light and power can also be generated

Not only does the IKAROS house not need power from an outside source, it actually generates extra energy that could be sold back to the local utility company.
LIVABLE HOME, GERMANY

from wind or water. More efficient systems for heating water and keeping homes warm in winter and cool in summer are constantly being developed. Some take advantage of heat stored deep within the Earth, and others use design features like wide overhangs and lots of ventilation to create airflow that speeds cooling. Heat energy from the sun or other sources can be captured and stored in thick walls and floors or used to heat water. Some in-floor heating systems use hot water running through buried pipes to keep rooms toasty during the colder months of the year.

Add a touch of innovation

It may not be practical to completely rebuild every house to make it more environmentally friendly, but there are many products—and more every day—intended to make houses more efficient.

An infrared photograph taken at night shows where a house is leaking heat. The white and red areas are the least energy efficient. The blue color of the roof shows that very little heat is being lost there, probably because the house has lots of insulation in this area. MANFRED SEREK

My Place

When I was in Iceland, I noticed that energy-efficient homes and buildings used readily available geothermal power as a heat source. In major cities like Reykjavik, the sidewalks are heated with hot water running beneath them. That means fewer people slip and get injured while walking on icy pathways. The house I was living in got its hot water straight from a natural hot spring! Getting hot water this way was extremely efficient, though its high sulfur content meant every shower smelled like rotten eggs! (DTS)

This hot water was as fresh as it comes, but included a unique smell!
DANI TATE-STRATTON

Smart thermostats learn when you're at home and adjust the temperature accordingly. Lights that turn off and on automatically, fridges that know when they've been left open and beep to alert you, window shades that raise and lower to keep temperatures stable, and even automatic feeding and watering stations to keep pets happy and healthy are all ways to automate your home and save energy. Who knows? Maybe one day houses will even know how to pick up your toys, fold your clothes and do your homework too!

WAYS OF LIVING TOGETHER

Families are constantly changing. Older relatives die, new babies are born, and young adults marry and start families of their own. Home designs change depending on who is planning to live together. In some places it's common for several generations of a family to live together. Extended families might share one large house or several smaller houses close together in a compound or on a farm. In other places it's more usual to find only parents and children living at the same address. In some cases, children of parents who no longer live together wind up having two homes.

INTENTIONAL COMMUNITIES

Sometimes, groups of people who are not related choose to purchase land together and create small communities in which people share responsibility for food production and farming, general upkeep of the property, and sometimes even running a business together. By working together and sharing skills and interests, people who live in communities like these (sometimes called intentional communities, communes, or co-housing projects) are able to pool their resources and help take care of each other.

When Dutch artists Haas&Hahn traveled to Brazil to paint this square in the community of Santa Marta, they trained twenty-five young residents to help them carry out the transformation. The project brought residents of the favela (shantytown) together and dramatically increased tourism in the area.
PEETER VIISIMAA/GETTY.COM

Many hands make light work! Traditional barn raisings allow farm families to build much larger and more complicated structures than they would be able to do on their own. IAN ADAMS

Older people might not need a large house after their families have grown up and moved away but may still be fit and well enough to live independently. Having others close by who can help with certain tasks an older person might find difficult is one benefit, but just as important is having a group of people to socialize with, share meals and provide companionship.

BARN RAISING

It wasn't so long ago that when a family needed a new barn all the neighbors would come together to help build it. If enough people shared the workload, it was possible to build a large structure in a very short amount of time. After the job was done, everyone enjoyed a delicious meal, music and dancing.

My Place

The first natural building at One United Resource (O.U.R.) Ecovillage was the Sanctuary, which features several styles of natural building. It's also energy efficient, has a green roof and has features like heated benches built of cob that funnel hot air from behind the fireplace. When Dani and I were writing this book, we stayed in the Sanctuary and had a chance to experience what it's like to live in a uniquely modern building built using ancient methods. (NT)

The Sanctuary has built-in humidity monitors that are being used to learn how a natural building like this one holds up in a cool, wet, West Coast climate. O.U.R. ECOVILLAGE

Community members can also get together to help build a house. Organizations like Habitat for Humanity coordinate volunteers (including the future home owners), accept donations of building materials and oversee projects that result in homes being built for a fraction of what it would cost to pay professionals. Sometimes projects like these also take advantage of used building materials that are salvaged when an old building is taken down.

SHELTER FOR EVERYONE

Whether miles above the Earth or deep underground, people have been adapting their homes to local living conditions, cultures and building materials for centuries. As the population of our planet continues to grow, creative architects, designers and builders will keep exploring new ways to provide comfortable, affordable housing for everyone. With advances in technology, homes of the future are likely to be more energy efficient and better suited to our changing climate and the needs of future generations of families and communities.

Perhaps new urban housing developments will include spaces for small farms the way cities and towns now include parkland. Maybe the homes of the future will be portable, expandable or able to warn residents when a roof is due to be replaced or the drains need cleaning. Maybe it will be very unusual for people to go out to work or school every day because our houses will be so interconnected technologically we'll be able to do more and more without ever setting foot outside.

When you grow up, what do you think your home might be like? It's fun to imagine how housing will change in the future, but just as it always has, a home will provide a safe place for people to sleep, share meals, socialize and raise a family.

Working with Habitat for Humanity is a great way to learn carpentry skills while helping a family in need. These students are volunteering in Albany, Georgia. HABITAT FOR HUMANITY/ STEFFAN HACKER

Resources

Websites

Airplane Hotel: www.costaverde.com

Coober Pedey: www.cooberpedy.sa.gov.au

Green Roof: www.greenroofplants.com

Habitat for Humanity: www.habitat.ca

Hostelling International: www.hihostels.com

How to Build an Igloo: (Classic Short Film) www.nfb.ca/film/how_to_build_an_igloo

How to Build a Tipi: tinyurl.com/fp-tipi

International Space Station: tinyurl.com/fp-iss

Kandovan: tinyurl.com/fp-kandovan

Mongolian Gers: www.mongolyurt.com

Mushroom Insulation: www.ecovativedesign.com

Natural Building: tinyurl.com/fp-natural-building

Odd Hotels: www.unusualhotelsoftheworld.com

O.U.R. Ecovillage: http://ourecovillage.org

Phuktal Monastery School: tinyurl.com/fp-monastery

Romany Vardo: http://gypsywaggons.co.uk

School Bus Conversions: www.skoolie.net

Solar Electric Light Fund (SELF): www.self.org

Spherical Tree Houses: www.freespiritspheres.com

Swedish Ice Hotel: www.icehotel.com

The World: http://aboardtheworld.com

United Nations Refugee Agency: www.unhcr.ca

Acknowledgments

Thank you, Nikki, for not only getting me into—and then through—this project, but also for being a pretty great mom, friend and co-adventurer. Toryn, thanks always for the endless love and support, the planning and scheming. I can't wait for us to grow into our goals together. Grumpy Grampy, thanks for being my biggest cheerleader underneath it all—always. Brandy, Trent, Freya and everyone else at the Village: thank you for welcoming me into your community with open arms. Also, of course, huge gratitude for opening the Sanctuary as a writing retreat—a better place to craft a book about natural building would be hard to find indeed. *Haichka*. To all the baristas at the Broadmead Starbucks, my home office away from home, thank you for keeping me caffeinated—none of my projects would happen without you! Finally, a huge thanks to Sarah Harvey and everyone else at Orca for the amazing work you do for Canadian publishing on the whole, and our little slice of it as well. I couldn't ask for a better home for my first book. (DTS)

Oh, Sarah Harvey, where would I be without you? There was a time, long ago, when I wondered why so many writers thanked their editors so profusely in the acknowledgments... Now I know. The rest of the team at Orca is not to be forgotten, of course—many thanks to everyone who is involved in the process from start to finish. Without my extraordinary family I would not be able to continue to live and work as I do—thank you to each one of you for your ongoing, steadfast support and encouragement. Dani, it has been a pleasure to work on this project with you and I hope it is just the first of many we tackle together! (NT)

A little color goes a long way toward making this neighborhood in Trancoso, Brazil, bright and cheerful. YADID LEVY/CORBIS.COM

Index

Index (continued)